GALAXY OF SUPERSTARS

Ben Affleck

Backstreet Boys

Garth Brooks

Mariah Carey

Cameron Diaz

Leonardo DiCaprio

Tom Hanks

Hanson

Jennifer Love Hewitt

Lauryn Hill

Ewan McGregor

Mike Myers

'N Sync

LeAnn Rimes

Britney Spears

Spice Girls

Jonathan Taylor Thomas

Venus Williams

CHELSEA HOUSE PUBLISHERS

GALAXY OF SUPERSTARS

'N Sync

John F. Grabowski

CHELSEA HOUSE PUBLISHERS
Philadelphia

Frontis: *Clockwise from top left, the quintet of 'N Sync—Justin, Chris, J.C., Lance, and Joey—are the pop-music sensation of the late 1990s.*

Produced by
21st Century Publishing and Communications, Inc.
New York, New York
http://www.21cpc.com

CHELSEA HOUSE PUBLISHERS

Editor in Chief: Stephen Reginald
Managing Editor: James D. Gallagher
Production Manager: Pamela Loos
Art Director: Sara Davis
Director of Photography: Judy L. Hasday
Senior Production Editor: LeeAnne Gelletly
Publishing Coordinator/Project Editor: James McAvoy
Assistant Editor: Anne Hill
Cover Designer: Keith Trego

Front Cover Photo: Anthony Cutajar/London Features Int'l
Back Cover Photo: Jen Lowery/London Features Int'l

The Chelsea House World Wide Web address is
http://www.chelseahouse.com

First Printing

1 3 5 7 9 8 6 4 2

Library of Congress Cataloging-in-Publication Data

Grabowski, John F.
  'N Sync / John F. Grabowski.
     p.   cm. – (Galaxy of superstars)
  Includes bibliographical references (p.   ) and index.
  Summary: Provides background on the five individual members of the
popular boy band, 'N Sync, and discusses the recent success of this group.
  ISBN 0-7910-5493-4 (hc). — ISBN 0-7910-5494-2 (pb)
  1. 'N Sync (Musical group)—Juvenile literature. 2. Singers —United States—
Biography—Juvenile literature. [1. 'N Sync (Musical group). 2. Singers.]
I. Title. II. Series.
ML3930.N3G73   1999
782.42184'092'2—dc21
[b]   99—40636
                                                                 CIP
                                                                 AC

CONTENTS

1

DISNEY
IN CONCERT

Being successful in show business, as in any field, is a combination of talent, hard work, and luck. The five young men known as 'N Sync—Chris Kirkpatrick, J.C. Chasez, Joey Fatone, Lance Bass, and Justin Timberlake—always had confidence in their talent. In the three years since Chris had formed the group in 1995, the boys had spent all their spare time fine-tuning their skills, practicing their singing and dancing for countless hours, day after day, week after week, month after month.

Their diligence had already paid off in spectacular fashion. They signed a contract with BMG, one of the largest record companies in the world, and became a major hit in Germany. All across Europe, Asia, and Australia, thousands of fans flocked to see 'N Sync. With their clean good looks and singing and dancing abilities, the fabulous five were one of the most engaging acts to hit the pop scene in years.

Despite their immense European popularity, however, the boys had yet to make a splash in their homeland.

Disney's Magic Kingdom is in Orlando, entertainment capital of Florida. Orlando is also the home base of 'N Sync. Already popular in Europe, the young singers and dancers gained nationwide fans in America when they performed for the Disney In Concert *television series.*

Europe was at the forefront of the "boy band" phenomenon. The Backstreet Boys, to whom 'N Sync was often compared, had only recently begun to make a name for itself in the United States. Backstreet Boys had also enjoyed early success in Germany.

The time seemed right for 'N Sync to break into the American market. The quintet's first single, "I Want You Back," was released in February of 1998. The song received a great deal of play on radio stations across the country and won the group many fans, particularly among teenage girls. The fact that the five young men were all attractive, as well as talented, did not hurt their chances. However, as Lou Pearlman of Trans Continental Entertainment says, "You have to be able to sing first or it doesn't matter how good-looking you are."

The group's first album was released soon after the single, and it too had all the earmarks of a hit. The boys began playing shows around the United States and had just finished a concert at the Mall of America in Minneapolis, Minnesota. 'N Sync was on a roll. The guys' music was catching on, and they were gathering new fans everywhere they performed.

Now, an unexpected bit of luck came their way. The Backstreet Boys had been scheduled to film a *Disney in Concert* special for the Disney Channel. The concert, to be filmed over the Memorial Day weekend at the Disney-MGM Studios, was to coincide with the opening of Animal Kingdom at Walt Disney World in Orlando, Florida.

Plans do not always work out as expected, however. The Backstreet Boys canceled at the last moment, and 'N Sync was invited to fill

in. The boys jumped at the chance. It was a tremendous opportunity for the group, which had made Orlando its base of operations.

On the Friday before the concert, the studio treated the boys and their families to a tour of the newest Disney attraction, followed by a press conference with members of the media at the Rainforest Cafe. Next, the five gave an interview for the Disney Channel. Afterwards, the boys had some free time to enjoy the park with their families before going home to rest up for the next day's performance. They took in the safari ride and the "Countdown to

As one of the hottest pop groups, the young men of 'N Sync combine their mellow harmonizing with dancing and exuberant gestures to thrill audiences worldwide.

Extinction" in Disney's latest spectacle.

Saturday began with a ceremony in which the boys set their handprints in cement in Disney's Walk of Fame. This ritual is a takeoff of the famous attraction outside Mann's Chinese Theater in Hollywood, California, but in Orlando it features entertainers who have connections with Disney.

Another press conference followed in the Beauty and the Beast Amphitheater, this one for 'N Sync's fans. Knowing how important their fans were to their success, the boys went out of their way to accommodate their admirers whenever possible. When one brave fan asked, "Today's my friend's birthday. Can you sing 'Happy Birthday' to her?" the boys did not miss a beat. They immediately chimed in with an impromptu version of "Happy Birthday to You," treating the young girl to a birthday memory she will undoubtedly cherish for years to come.

The five boys spent the remainder of the time in last-minute preparations for the concert. As they performed, mixing in songs from their album with some new arrangements, they did not disappoint their audience. Energized by the large crowd, the five put on one of their best shows, harmonizing and dancing, and their fans loved every minute of it.

By the time the evening was over, Chris, Joey, J.C., Justin, and Lance knew the concert had been a success. They did not realize just how much of a success, however. "Even after we filmed it," recalled Chris, "we just thought it was a little concert. I was like, 'Well, that was cool. Now we gotta go work on our careers.'"

On July 18, the show was televised on the Disney Channel as part of the *In Concert* series. Other shows in the series, featuring performers such as LeAnn Rimes and Brandy, had done very well, but 'N Sync received the highest ratings of all. Because of popular demand, the show was repeated several times.

The exposure brought the group countless numbers of new fans. Appearing on television could truly be said to have put them over the top. Those familiar with the boys' singing talents had their first exposure to the group's dancing prowess. Candid footage of the five and their families was included in the show, giving viewers the opportunity to get to know them a little more intimately.

Because of the Disney show, 'N Sync was no longer just a name on a CD label. The band was now a group of five likable young men ready to make their mark in their homeland, just as they already had in countries around the globe. They were talented, hip young singers and dancers who could thrill fans of all ages with their dancing abilities onstage as well as with their vocal talents. The boys had created a group with whom millions of fans the world over are "in sync."

2

THE BOYS
OF 'N SYNC

Looking back on it now, it does not seem surprising that Christopher "Chris" Alan Kirkpatrick was the inspiration for the musical group 'N Sync. Coming into the world in the small town of Clarion, Pennsylvania, on October 17, 1971, Chris was the first child born to a family with a long musical tradition. His mom, Beverly, and her brothers, sister, parents, and grandparents were all involved with music in one way or another. As she relates, "Everyone in my family is a musician. So saying that you want to put together a band in my family is a lot like telling somebody you want to learn to ride a bike in someone else's family. It's real normal."

Young Chris revealed his talent at a very early age. His mother used to sing the hymn "Coventry Carol" to put him to sleep at night when he was an infant. One day she overheard him mimicking the tune, although he was too young to speak the words.

Chris's dad died when the boy was still young, and his mom remarried. When the family moved to Dayton,

---

Chris Kirkpatrick displayed musical talent from an early age, singing, playing piano and guitar, and appearing in school musical productions. Determined to pursue a musical career, he performed at Universal Studios in Orlando, where he got the idea for the a cappella group 'N Sync.

Ohio, Chris became involved in school stage productions. He began taking piano as well as guitar and voice lessons in an effort to develop his musical talents. He also earned a reputation as one of the funniest kids in school, willing to do anything for a laugh. Chris once gave a moving performance in his high school's production of *South Pacific*. When it was time to take his bow, he walked out on the stage— in a hula skirt and coconut bra!

In addition to being serious about his music, Chris was also serious about his studies. After graduating from high school, he moved on to Valencia College in Dayton to continue his education. Although he began by majoring in theater, he soon switched over to music and psychology. When Chris was not attending classes, he sang with the school choir and also performed with groups at coffeehouses in the Dayton area.

After earning his associate of arts degree, Chris made a decision that would have a major impact on his life. Determined to get his bachelor's degree, he moved to Florida to attend Rollins College. Money soon became a problem, however, and the young student found work singing with a group called the Caroling Company. Through some members of the group, he heard that auditions were being held for the chance to perform at Universal Studios in Orlando.

This was the opportunity Chris was looking for. He passed the audition with flying colors and landed a part with the Hollywood High Tones (his name was Spike), a doo-wop group. "We used to sing outside the Fifties diner at Universal," explains Chris. "That was me—it was three guys and one girl and we'd sing

Fifties a cappella music [singing without instrumental accompaniment]."

Because of his job at Universal, full-time study at Rollins was impossible. Chris had made a decision, however, and he knew he could only be happy by putting all his energy into his music. After eventually dropping out of school, he concentrated on polishing his craft at Universal.

There were no performers in Joshua Scott "J.C." Chasez's family, but the son of Roy and Karen Chasez still had a great deal of exposure to music. Born in Washington, D.C., on August 8, 1976, baby Joshua loved to move to the sounds he heard coming from the radio. Since dancing seemed to appeal so much to the boy, when the family moved to nearby Bowie, Maryland, Karen signed her son up for dance lessons.

Although the lessons helped improve the youngster's self-confidence, he was still too shy to perform on a stage. If it had not been for an incident that occurred when he was 12 years old, young J.C. might never have become the performer he is today.

One day while he was at his friend Kacy's house, a couple of girls they knew stopped by. The two boys had reputations as good dancers, and the girls wanted to enter a talent contest with them. Although reluctant at first, J.C. agreed to go along after his friend dared him. The foursome proceeded to take first prize in the contest. "Even though I did it because I was dared to," reports J.C., "I was happy that we won. We did it a couple more times, and wherever we went, we won first place; we were taking all the ribbons. I just did it for kicks."

Joshua "J.C." Chasez, an alumnus of The Mickey Mouse Club, *grew up in a family that surrounded him with music. Dedicated to his music, J.C. is known as a workaholic whose vocal talents with different musical styles help make 'N Sync's sound so special.*

Around this time, Karen Chasez spotted an item in the local newspaper that would change J.C.'s life. *The Mickey Mouse Club* (MMC) was going to be holding auditions in the Washington area. J.C. agreed to try out and was selected as one of the 12 finalists out of 500 who showed up. After further auditions in Los Angeles, J.C. was offered a job on the show. "Disney auditioned twenty thousand kids in the United States and Canada that year," says his mom. "They hired ten, and he was one of them."

J.C. moved to Orlando with his dad while his mom and younger brother and sister remained in Maryland. Over the next four years, he honed his acting and dancing skills with the show, which was also the launching pad for singer Britney Spears and actress Keri Russell of *Felicity*. In the program's weekly drama—*Emerald Cove*—he played the part of Clarence "Wipeout" Adams.

With the encouragement of his dance instructor, J.C. also began to sing and eventually performed some solos on the show. As J.C. remembers, "I didn't start singing until I got to Orlando with *The Mickey Mouse Club*. I didn't know that much about music. I just knew that I liked to dance and I started singing cover tunes." Bitten by the bug, J.C. knew he wanted to pursue his singing.

Born in Brooklyn, New York, on January 28, 1977, to Phyllis and Joseph Fatone, little Joseph Anthony Fatone Jr. liked to make believe he was Superman. As a result, his tiny body took quite a pounding. "The emergency room staff knew him by his first name," laughs his father. Luckily, Joey's attempts at singing met with more success than his attempts at flying. In this he took after his dad, Joe Sr., who once sang with a doo-wop group called the Orions.

Joey sang and danced and performed in church plays and musicals. The outgoing youngster loved the feeling he got when he performed in front of an audience. "I thought it was the greatest feeling to get applause," he explains, "to get to feed off the audience. I loved being onstage and watching people's faces. I still like getting that response."

At age seven, Joey even appeared as an

Introduced to music and theater by his parents, Joey Fatone sang and danced at Universal Studios in Orlando when he was a teenager. There he met Chris, who wanted Joey's baritone-tenor voice to enhance 'N Sync's harmonizing vocal style.

extra in the Sergio Leone film *Once Upon a Time in America*, which starred Robert De Niro. When Joey was 13 years old, his family relocated to Orlando. His talent for performing came in handy in helping him make new friends. "My family wanted to move to Florida," says Joey. "It's sunny all the time and nice. The houses were a little bit cheaper and there was actually more space."

It was in Florida that the teen improved his dancing skills through formal lessons. "In high school," says Joey, "when I tried to do musicals, that's when I pretty much got involved with dancing. I took a little bit of jazz, a little ballet, I *tried* to do tap but . . ."

Joey continued acting outside of school and appeared as an extra in *Matinee*, a 1993 film starring John Goodman. He also made a brief appearance in an episode of the television series *SeaQuest*. Despite these movie and television credits, however, Joey still got his biggest rush from performing in front of a live audience onstage.

After graduating from Orlando's Dr. Phillips High School in 1995, Joey secured a job at Universal Studios. "I did a show called *The Beetlejuice Graveyard Review*," he recalls, "and I played characters like the Wolfman and Dracula." It was the perfect position for the young performer. Where else could he get paid for doing what he enjoyed most—singing and dancing and making people happy?

Joey's love of entertaining was shared by another Universal employee with whom he had become friends, a boy by the name of Chris Kirkpatrick.

When James Lance Bass was a child, he dreamed of being an astronaut. Little did the boy realize that one day he would soar into the stratosphere in an entirely different way.

Born in Clinton, Mississippi, on May 4, 1979, to Jim and Diane Bass, Lance grew up with a love of music and gave evidence of his talent early on. As soon as he was old enough, he began singing with a children's choir. "I grew up singing in church," recalls Lance, "and I always loved singing." By the time he reached the eighth grade, he had auditioned for—and won— a spot with the Mississippi Show Stoppers, the statewide chorus. A year later, Lance began working with a voice coach in order to help him make the most of his gift.

When the chance came to join a show choir called Attache, Lance did not hesitate. He began touring the country with the group, which repeatedly won competitions, establishing a reputation as one of the best show choirs in the United States. Included in the group's repertoire were several choreographed routines. "That's where I really learned how to sing and dance," says Lance. He fell right into place and added dance lessons to his busy schedule.

For the first time in his life, Lance began to consider the field of entertainment as a possible career. The matter was clinched for him after seeing a concert that featured country singer Garth Brooks. "I was fourteen," he reports. "I thought his show was incredible. I thought, 'That's what I want to do.'"

As a senior in high school, Lance's immediate future included college. He had already been accepted at the University of Nebraska. He could not have known that his plans were about to change dramatically. College would have to wait.

Growing up in a city with a long musical heritage, it is not surprising that Justin Randall Timberlake seemed to have music in his blood. The blond, blue-eyed youngster was born to Randy and Lynn Timberlake in Memphis, Tennessee, on January 31, 1981. His father played bluegrass, so young Justin was around music all the time. "Justin has always, always exhibited great talent for music," confides his mother. "From when he was a tiny baby, not walking or talking yet,

As a boy in Clinton, Mississippi, Lance Bass loved to perform and sang and danced in show choirs. In addition to his musical talents, he brings his interest in management, describing himself as "the business one of the group."

when he was three to four months old, you could turn music on and he would always keep time with the music, kicking to the beat of the music."

While still only a toddler, Justin's parents divorced. He stayed with his mother, who eventually remarried. One constant in the youngster's early life was his participation in church activities, like other 'N Sync members. As soon as he was old enough, Justin began to sing with the other members of the congregation.

Although the youngest member of 'N Sync, Justin Timberlake is the show-business veteran of the group. He toured with local school shows, entered amateur contests, and was a performer on Star Search, *and* The Mickey Mouse Club *before teaming up with 'N Sync.*

"I come from a big background of family singers, singing in church," says Justin. "My grandmother, my daddy, my uncles, my aunts, I got it from them." As the young singer gained experience, he started entering—and winning —local talent shows, including a Dance Like the New Kids on the Block contest.

When Justin learned that the producers of

the television show *Star Search* were coming to
Memphis, he jumped at the chance to audition
for them. He was chosen to appear on the show,
which was filmed in Orlando. Although Justin
did not win *Star Search*, his trip to Florida was
not a total loss. As luck would have it, *The
Mickey Mouse Club* was being taped on the very
next soundstage. Justin found out that in the
near future the show would be holding auditions in Nashville, Tennessee, only a few hours
by car from Memphis. He attended the tryouts
and eventually was selected as one of the new
cast members of *The Mickey Mouse Club*.

For Justin, being on the show was a dream
come true. He was a big fan of the program
and was thrilled to have the opportunity to
perform. "By far, it's one of the best things
I've ever done in my whole life," he recalls.
"I couldn't have thought of a better thing to
do. You get to dip your fingers into everything.
You're not restricted to one thing at all. Doing
the comedy was a lot of fun. You weren't
restricted to one kind of music."

Justin's dream lasted two years before the
show's run ended. As often happens in life,
however, when one door closes, another one
opens. Justin would walk through the next
door together with his close friend from the
show, J.C. Chasez.

3

PRACTICE
MAKES PERFECT

Chris Kirkpatrick formulated his plan for starting an a cappella group in 1995, while he was working at Universal. He contacted Justin, whom he had known from an audition in Orlando, and Justin brought in fellow *Mickey Mouse Club* alumnus J.C. When Joey, whom Chris had come to know as a colleague at Universal (and a one-time extra who danced the closing song on *MMC*), joined the trio, the core of the group was in place. "Everybody knew each other in a roundabout way," says J.C., "it was just a matter of the order that everybody called each other. But, Chris was the one who came up with the idea of the group."

The boys realized they had their work cut out for them. Thousands of groups across the country are trying to make it in the music business, but success does not come easily. Each of the four boys was willing to do whatever was necessary to fulfill his dream.

They began rehearsing whenever they had free time, usually for several hours in the evening. "When we had no record company, no management, when we first

---

Once 'N Sync was formed, the five boys practiced and rehearsed for hundreds of hours, perfecting their unique vocal harmonizing and dancing style. When they got their big break with a European record company, the boys began their incredible rise in the pop-music world.

started and we were just rehearsing," relates Joey, "I was still working, and I would go to work during the day and rehearse at night, from nine to midnight. It took a lot of hard work, dedication, and some sacrifices."

Even at this early stage, the foursome, whose voices blended together perfectly, knew they were on the right track. One element was missing, however. They needed another voice for the bass parts in order to round out their sound. Where could they find someone to fill that role?

Since none of the group knew anyone he could recommend, each began making calls, including one to Justin's old vocal coach in Memphis. The coach suggested another one of his students—Lance Bass—whom the boys contacted.

Agreeing to give it a try, Lance flew to Florida and sang with the group. Right away, the others knew he was the one. "They just flew me down," remembers Lance, "and I met them and joined that day. We sang 'The Star-Spangled Banner' together, or something like that, and that was it." Lance's voice blended in perfectly, and when his parents agreed to let him join the group, the last piece of the puzzle had been put in place.

The boys knew they needed someone to oversee the group. "For the first year we were together we were struggling to find management," remembers J.C. When Justin's mom, Lynn, offered her assistance, one of the first things she did was help them decide on a name. One day, she happened to mention how "in sync" they seemed to be, since their voices and dancing blended together so well. As Lance reports, ". . . our big forte is our harmonies. That's the reason we chose 'N Sync as our name, because we love to do everything a cappella."

They later realized that 'N Sync was almost

an acronym for the last letters of their first names—N for Justin, S for Chris, Y for Joey, and C for J.C. What they still needed was another N. To make the names fit, Justin began calling Lance "Lansten," and a nickname was born.

With the group complete, the five threw themselves into their work. They spent hundreds of hours rehearsing and practicing in a hot, steamy warehouse in Orlando, where they all lived together with Justin's mom. Finally, they were ready to make their move.

At Lynn's suggestion, they put together a demo package to send to prospective managers. The package, consisting of a CD, a video, and posters, was entirely the work of the group. A friend of theirs had taped the video of the group's performances at Disney World's Pleasure Island. They invested their own money in the project. As Chris remembers, ". . . it was all done by us—the printing of the posters, the choosing of the outfits, the song orders, the choreography—everything. It was a lot of work."

In early 1996, the package reached the offices of Lou Pearlman in Orlando. Pearlman was the man who had discovered—and invested in—the Backstreet Boys, the group to whom 'N Sync would often be compared. Originally, Pearlman had been involved in the transportation field, leasing jets to acts like Michael Jackson and Paul McCartney. That initial brush with show business made him eager for more. He became an entertainment investor, financially backing acts he believed would be successful.

Pearlman liked what he heard and saw and immediately contacted his partner, Johnny Wright, who was in Germany at the time. Wright, who had previously been involved with New Kids on the Block, flew back to Orlando,

Looking like young astronauts, the boys practice their routine onstage. Appearing onstage gave the group experience in performing before live audiences and helped get their name out.

where he heard the boys sing. He was very impressed. "They could really sing," said Wright. "They had a chemistry—an aura about them. When they talked to me, they talked to me as a group, as a unit, rather than five individuals trying to pitch themselves to me—they weren't selfish."

The two men sat down with the five boys, Justin's mom, and Lance's parents. They arrived at a deal: Pearlman would supply the financial backing, and Wright would become the group's manager. 'N Sync was on its way.

Although the boys had been practicing together for several months, they still had a way to go before they were ready to sign with a record company. They continued to practice and also began appearing at small shows in the Orlando area. The five were able to try out some new dance moves they had developed while working with choreographer Robert Jacquez. One of the best in the business, Jacquez had worked with Michael Jackson, among others.

Performing in front of a live crowd also had another benefit. The boys saw the effect their vocalizing and dancing had on others, something they could not experience in a recording studio. They had always been confident in their abilities, but seeing smiling faces and hearing applause reinforced that confidence. They knew they had the talent to make others happy with their music, and that was their driving force. As Justin puts it, "I love the feeling when you're up there onstage singing and the crowd is getting into what you are doing. I love to see smiles on their faces and know that I had something to do with that."

In the meantime, Pearlman and Wright were also busy. At that time, in 1996, boy bands and pop music were not yet big in the United States. After signing on to manage the Backstreet Boys, Wright had decided to have that group make its start in the European market. His judgment proved to be on target. Backstreet Boys were a smash hit in Europe, where the Spice Girls, among others, were also filling the airways with pop music.

Wright now decided on the same plan of action for 'N Sync. With his contacts overseas, he soon had BMG in Germany ready to offer the boys a deal. The five signed contracts with BMG Ariola Munich, and within days the boys were on a plane heading for Germany. The quick turn of events did not faze the young men. As Justin recalls, "We were, like, we don't care where you take us—we just want to sing!" And, as they were to soon find out, Germany was ready to hear them.

4

A SMASH HIT
IN EUROPE

The boys were based in Munich for the next year and a half, but their travels would soon take them far and wide. The first order of business was to gather together a team of producers, songwriters, and arrangers. Johnny Wright quickly enlisted the services of producers Denniz Pop and Max Martin. In past years, this duo had teamed together with the Backstreet Boys, Robyn, and Ace of Bass. Their track record was quite impressive. Other arrangers, producers, and songwriters were enlisted, including Gary Carolla, Christian Hamm, Kristian Lundin, Veit Renn, and Full Force.

The boys flew to Stockholm, Sweden, to record two songs at Pop's Cheiron Studios. The resulting tunes— "I Want You Back" and "Tearin' Up My Heart"—would be 'N Sync's first two single releases. At the same time, others were working behind the scenes to put together the material for the group's first album. These preparations required the boys to fly back and forth to Orlando, where they recorded at Lou Pearlman's Trans Continental studio or at Parc or House of Hits studios.

Like many of the boy bands of the '90s, 'N Sync established its foothold on the pop-music world in Europe. Based in Munich, Germany, for more than a year, the boys recorded hit singles, toured the country, and received an enthusiastic reception.

'N Sync's work quickly paid off. "I Want You Back" was released in Germany in September 1996 and immediately became a hit. As J.C. would describe it, "The song is about suddenly finding yourself separated from the person you feel so deeply about because you've done something stupid to screw it up. I think it hits [people] because they can relate to it like a love song, but it's powerful and up tempo enough to kick them too." The song broke Michael Jackson's record by becoming Germany's fastest-rising single ever.

BMG President Thomas Stein marveled, "I have hardly ever witnessed newcomers enter the German charts with such incredible, rocket-like speed." Although the tune never actually reached the number one spot, it remained on the charts long enough to sell more than 350,000 copies, a phenomenal number for a country the size of Germany.

When "Tearin' Up My Heart" was released a couple of months later, it too became a hit. It reached the number 10 spot on the charts, also selling more than 350,000 copies. Staying at the top is often said to be harder than reaching it in the first place. Many groups in the past had enjoyed one hit song and were never heard from again. By following up with a second hit, 'N Sync proved it was not a one-hit wonder. The boys were developing a fan base who loved their sound and would buy future recordings. That base was fast spreading beyond Germany's borders as more songs were released—and became hits—in Austria, Holland, Hungary, Sweden, and Switzerland.

With their singles receiving increasing airtime, the plan was for the group to hit the road for a 17-date tour of Germany. 'N Sync's

popularity had reached such heights that concerts quickly sold out. Fans were anxious to get their first chance to see the boys in person.

The tour had several objectives. First, it allowed more people to hear the group's music. The more people heard 'N Sync's songs, the more likely it was that they would become fans and buy the boys' album when it was released later in the year.

Second, the tour helped fans get to know the boys themselves. By seeing them perform on stage, admirers could connect faces and personalities to the voices they were familiar with from the radio. The result, hopefully, would help audiences develop a bond with the group.

Aside from the marketing aspects, the tour would also give 'N Sync an opportunity to develop its stage act. Fans had heard how well the boys could sing. Now, they could also see how well the group could dance and perform.

The "Gang of Five" shows fans their dancing prowess. Part of what separates 'N Sync from other boy bands is their energetic action onstage.

A final reason for the tour was to give Chris, Joey, J.C., Justin, and Lance a taste of what they would face in the future. Traveling from one city to another and performing every night can be extremely tiring, and facing the media day after day can be mentally exhausting. The tour would give the boys some hint as to what their lives would be like as they became more famous.

When faced with a grueling schedule, it often helps if performers develop a routine that prepares them to face each day. During the course of the tour, the boys came up with two rituals they performed before each show. The first was a quick game of Hacky Sack to help loosen them up and ease the tension. Of course this could present other problems. "We have to delay the show sometimes," reports Lance, "because we're not very good."

The other ritual is one that helps the group prepare mentally. All five of the boys have strong religious beliefs. Just prior to the start of a show, they gather together with their road crew for a moment of prayer. "Without praying," they all concur, "we wouldn't dare to take a step on the stage."

The mini-tour was a resounding success. Mobs of fans came out to see the group at every stop along the way. Young women screamed out their names whenever they appeared in public. The boys finally had to travel with bodyguards wherever they went.

Ironically, while on tour the group happened to meet up with the Spice Girls, who were largely responsible for the "pop music" wave 'N Sync was following. The encounter occurred at an airport in Germany where the two groups were waiting to catch flights. "They didn't have security and we didn't have security," recalled

Chris. "We met them in the airport and we just sat down and talked with them." The tour was just the beginning, however. In May 1997, 'N Sync's first album was ready for release. A new tour was scheduled, this one to take the boys all across the continent of Europe.

European fans could not get enough. Not only did fans have the boys' singles, but MTV Europe and Viva! (a German version of MTV) were airing videos of the group's first two hits. Their popularity on the rise, the boys were in constant demand for interviews and photo shoots. They flew from city to city, laying the groundwork for their upcoming tour.

Scheduled for release in Germany on May 26, the boys' first album, *'N Sync,* had already surpassed the 250,000 mark in advance sales. *'N Sync* broke into the charts at number 22 and then quickly shot up to the top position. It was the first 'N Sync recording to reach the number one spot and also made the top-10 in Austria, Holland, Hungary, Sweden, and Switzerland.

Fourteen songs were included on *'N Sync.* The songs were the creations of several writers and producers and covered a wide range of styles. "I Want You Back," the up-tempo, catchy tune that was the group's first hit single, is about a ruined love affair. "Tearin' Up My Heart" is the addictive follow-up single about another frustrated relationship. "For the Girl Who Has Everything" and "Sailing" are ballads that beautifully demonstrate the boys' harmonizing talents. The latter is a remake of the Christopher Cross hit of 1980—and one of Joey's dad's favorite songs.

"More Than a Feeling" is an updated version of a 1976 hit by the group Boston. The boys sang it in their own inimitable style, and the

Adoring fans line up for autographs from their idols. The boys of 'N Sync don't hesitate to show their appreciation to their crowds of fans, who have helped make the group an international hit.

song came across as a tuneful ballad rather than the hard-rock original interpretation. That song is one of five that appeared on the European version of *'N Sync* but which would not appear on the album later released in the United States. The other four in that category are "Riddle," "Best of My Life," "Together Again," and "Forever Young." The last is not the Rod Stewart hit but rather an inspirational ditty about prevailing against all odds. "Forever Young" had a special meaning for the boys since it symbolized their own road to stardom.

The remaining songs included the sentimental love song "I Need Love," an upbeat dance tune, "You Got It", and the song "Crazy for You," which is a kind of mixture of several styles. "Here We Go," which was released as a single and would rise to number eight in Germany, is one of the most popular songs at the boys' concerts. The number is like a sing-along, with the audience answering the five's

cry of "Here we go" by responding, "'N Sync
has got the flow!"

The album's final cut, "Giddy Up," is Chris's
favorite since it was cowritten by the boys
together with Veit Renn. "I can remember
when we were in the studio writing that," he
recalls, "and how much fun it was to write with
the guys."

The many months of practice and rehearsals
were well worth the effort. Backed by a seven-
piece band, the boys began the tour, performing
the songs from their new album, accompanied
by their signature dance athletics. 'N Sync was
truly a European sensation, winning the hearts
of fans everywhere they performed. The tour
proved to be exhausting, however. "We tour so
hard," reported Justin. "We've toured for a
month straight, city after city, and we'd get
maybe two days off the entire tour. I had never
experienced touring to the point that you
started losing weight!"

Touring can also have its dangers. At one
stop along the way, Justin broke his thumb
during a performance. "Somebody put some
water on the stage," he recalls. "We were doing
an outside show and they were hosing down
the audience. We do this dance move where we
slide across the stage and my hand buckled."

Despite such setbacks, success continued
to follow the group. When all was said and
done, the results could not have been more
positive. The boys' faith in themselves—and
Lou Pearlman's and Johnny Wright's—had not
been misplaced. With three hit singles, a
smash album, and a major tour under their
belts, the five headed back home to Florida for
some rest and relaxation.

5

BACK IN
THE USA

The boys returned home to find a resurgence of pop music in the United States. The Spice Girls and Hanson were winning countless fans among the younger set. When the Backstreet Boys hit the charts with their single "Quit Playing Games (With My Heart)," it appeared that the country might finally be ready to accept the "boy band" craze which had taken Europe by storm.

The five also came home with new looks. Being exposed to fashions and styles in Europe gave the boys a chance to express their personalities through changes in their appearances. Chris had allowed his hair to grow and now wore a small goatee. Joey also adopted the goatee look and had his hair cut shorter on the sides. J.C.'s hair was a little longer and his clothes a little sportier. Justin's curly locks were now bleached, and he too dressed more casually. Lance's most noticeable change was getting his blond hair spiked.

Another thing that changed was the way in which the five were received. They had gotten used to being mobbed everywhere they went overseas, but they were brought

Returning from Europe with some "new looks" to show off their individuality, the boys were ready to ride the resurgent wave of enthusiasm for boy bands in the United States. They began a hectic schedule of recording and preparing for another tour overseas.

back to reality when they found they could go wherever they wanted without being recognized or mobbed. The boys realized this was a good experience. "We consider it lucky that we hit in Europe and got so huge, but remained unknown in the States," remembered Justin. "It gave us the chance to sit back and digest what was happening as it happened. We might have gotten crazy about it, but then we'd come home and it was like a reality check."

'N Sync still had other commitments, however, before it could test the American musical waters. Because of their popularity, which was spreading like wildfire, the boys were scheduled for a promotional tour overseas. Their legions of fans were no longer confined to Europe. The group now had thousands of fans in Asia and Australia who were clamoring to see their idols.

Before heading for Asia, the group appeared on television, radio, and in all the print media in Europe. When they finally performed in the Far East, the boys found fans there to be every bit as avid as those elsewhere, but much more polite. The tour ended with a stop in Australia, where the band's popularity had also been established.

From the "Land Down Under," 'N Sync returned to the United States again. Another European jaunt was planned for early 1998, however, and the five had little time for relaxation. They began working on new songs and new dance routines for their next tour. In January, the group took to the highways and byways of Europe again, serenading their fans with their new act. For two months the boys entertained their adoring admirers, who never seemed to get enough of them.

When the band returned home this time, a

pleasant surprise was waiting for them. "I Want You Back" had been released in the United States on February 13. Within weeks, it had shown signs of being as big a hit here as it had been abroad. The video was getting a lot of play on MTV, and the song was on its way. America was finding out what much of the rest of the world already knew—'N Sync was indeed a force to be reckoned with.

Some critics, however, dismissed the group as nothing more than a clone of the Backstreet Boys. Others went so far as to call 'N Sync "Backstreet Boys lite." The two groups do, in fact, have much in common. They are both composed of five talented, good-looking young men, both were based in Orlando, and both were discovered and backed by Lou Pearlman's organization.

Wildly popular in Europe, the Backstreet Boys are one of the first of the boy bands. Although often compared to Backstreet, 'N Sync is uniquely different. Each of the 'N Sync five gives his own vocal sound to the group's melodious harmonizing, and their acrobatic dance moves also set them apart.

The boys and their fans, however, have learned not to worry about such negative notions. They view their dancing talents as one important difference between the two groups. "I think the choreography is really key," says Chris. "When you see our show, you'll see that we dance with every song—except for one a cappella song. When we sing, we like to dance, we like to move around and we show that onstage. There's even a dance break where all we do is dance. It's a lot of fun."

"I Want You Back" remained on the charts for six months, making it all the way up to number 13. The song sold more than a million copies and gave the boys memories they would never forget. "I heard the song on the radio on *Casey's Top 40*," Lance would later remark, "and it was weird, because we all grew up listening to Casey Kasem. It sounded so good!"

'N Sync was released by RCA Records a little more than a month after "I Want You Back" hit the stores. The album broke into *Billboard's* top 200 chart at number 40 and began its rise toward the top 10. As summer came, the album had sold more than a million copies and gone platinum. The American version of *'N Sync* included four songs not on the European release. "I Just Wanna Be with You" was the work of producers Full Force. A little funkier than most of the group's work, the song included a sample from Sly and the Family Stone's classic "Family Affair." "Everything I Own" was the boys' rendition of the 1970s soft-rock hit by Bread, while "I Drive Myself Crazy," later released as a single in Germany, was a soulful mixture of rhythm-and-blues and pop.

The last new track on the album was Justin's and Lance's favorite. "God Must Have Spent a

Little More Time on You" is a beautiful romantic ballad that would be the group's third single
released in the States. As Lance put it, ". . .
the words and melody are incredible. I get chill
bumps whenever I listen to it."

'N Sync fans with personal computers had
an additional surprise in store for them. *'N Sync*
is actually an enhanced CD, with several features that can be viewed on a computer. When
the disc is inserted into a computer's CD-ROM
drive, files can be opened that present bio-
graphical information about the boys, list
lyrics to the songs, and connect the user with
websites on the Internet. Users can also view
pictures and even a brief video.

Over the next several weeks, the boys spent
time on the road promoting the album and
getting ready for their first American tour. The
group's first concert of note was at the Mall of
America in Minneapolis, but the five's break-
through date was at Walt Disney World in
Orlando. When the Disney concert was broad-
cast on the Disney Channel that summer, the
'N Sync phenomenon truly took off.

Following the Disney concert, the boys ven-
tured to New York City for the first time. The
highlight of the trip to the Big Apple was a
concert sponsored by radio station Z100 to
raise money for charity. Staged at New York's
legendary Radio City Music Hall, the concert
included such performers as Mariah Carey,
Gloria Estefan, Olivia Newton-John, Paula Cole,
Third Eye Blind, and Matchbox 20. As the
review in *Billboard* reported, 'N Sync held its
own. "Among favorite moments for the sold-
out Radio City Music Hall crowd [was] . . . a
performance by 'N Sync, who danced and sang
like banshees amid throngs of mesmerized

The members of 'N Sync entertain enthusiastic fans at a charity concert run by Z100 in New York City. All of the guys enjoy performing at benefits, believing that it is important to give of their time and talents to help others.

and screaming girls."

The rest of the summer of '98 found the boys stepping up their hectic pace. They continued to make promotional appearances at stores, giving their fans a chance to meet them at every stop along the way. The media blitz snowballed as magazines such as *Billboard, Entertainment Weekly, Teen People, Seventeen, Teen Beat, Twist,* and *Tiger Beat* all clamored for interviews and photos. The boys' schedule of concert appearances took them north to Canada, where their fans were eager to have the chance to see them in person for the first time.

In August the five were back in the United

States performing at arenas, theme parks, state fairs, and malls. 'N Sync did not forget TV, either. The group was booked for appearances on both *The Tonight Show with Jay Leno* and *Live! With Regis & Kathie Lee.*

One of the boys' favorite kinds of performances were their charity concerts, such as the one run by Z100 in New York. "I think you just do as much as you can," said Chris to *Teen Beat* magazine. "When I was little, I tried to do as much as I could as often as I could. Now that we've got a name out there, it's a lot easier for us to do more for charity because you can appeal to the masses."

'N Sync headlined at the event called The Truth Train, on their home territory in Florida. This event, organized by Students Working Against Tobacco, tried to bring attention to the problem of teen smoking. Another concert in California was the Wango Tango benefit, which raised money for local organizations. "We played in a stadium and it was a huge rush to be on that stage in front of that many people," said J.C. "There was a good vibe because it was for a good cause too, so we enjoyed it."

As the summer neared its end, the boys made another promotional trip to New York. Entertainment mogul Richard Branson was opening a new Virgin Megastore in downtown Manhattan at the edge of Greenwich Village. 'N Sync was enlisted, along with other celebrities, to take part in the festivities. The highlight of the day was a double-decker bus ride from Times Square to the downtown store. Together with Branson, singer Petula Clark, and camera crews, the boys waved to fans and sang from the upper level of the bus as it moved through the streets of the city. Some lucky fans along

Crowds gather to watch and cheer as the boys ride through New York City to the opening of Virgin Records' megastore in downtown Manhattan.

the way were allowed to board the bus and meet their idols. It was the kind of opportunity the boys enjoyed—a chance to give a little something back to their fans.

Eventually, the boys returned home, but they found little time to rest up and relax. Over the next two weeks they recorded the vocals for 14 songs that were to be featured on their new album, due to be released in November. Their second album—*Home for Christmas*—consisted of a few old standards and some new Christmas tunes. Included among the traditional songs were "The First Noel," "O Holy Night," and the Mel Torme classic "The Christmas Song (Chestnuts Roasting on an Open Fire)."

The new holiday songs, many of which were produced by Veit Renn, included "Home for Christmas," "Under My Tree," "I Never Knew the Meaning of Christmas," "Merry Christmas, Happy Holidays," "I Guess It's Christmas Time," "All I Want Is You This Christmas," "In Love on Christmas," "It's Christmas," "Love's in Our Hearts on Christmas Day," "The Only Gift," and "Kiss Me at Midnight."

Home for Christmas was scheduled for release just prior to the start of their headlining tour. Before that, however, the boys would be spending two weeks performing as the opening act for Janet Jackson's *Velvet Rope* tour. This was a huge thrill for the group, especially for young Justin. "You don't understand how much I'm in love with Janet Jackson," he said. "Probably about two or three years ago I had her on my wall, so I'm pretty infatuated."

When November 10 rolled around, *Home for Christmas* hit the stores and immediately took off on the charts, making its first appearance on the *Billboard* charts at number seven. Meanwhile, *'N Sync* was still on the charts at number three. Incredibly, the boys had two albums in the top 10 at the same time! This almost unheard-of event proved beyond the shadow of a doubt what the group's fans already knew: the band that had smashed records in Europe was destined to be as big, if not bigger, in the United States. It was only a matter of time.

6

1999 AND
BEYOND

As the end of 1998 approached, Chris, J.C., Joey, Lance, and Justin had a couple of weeks to reflect on all that had happened in an amazing year. They took a break from their tour to return home and spend the Christmas holidays with their families. Looking back, it was difficult to grasp just how far 'N Sync had come in such a short time.

At the beginning of the year, the group was still largely unknown in the United States. The boys could walk around without having to worry about being besieged by fans wherever they went. Now, 12 months later, the five were being hailed as the best new group of the year.

The video for their hit single "I Want You Back" had won two *Billboard* Music Video Awards for them—as Best Clip of the Year and Best New Artist Clip of the Year in the dance-video category. They had two hit singles under their belts and two albums in the top 10. Amazingly, "God Must Have Spent a Little More Time on You" was receiving so much playing time on the radio that it had

---

The year 1999 was a triumph for the boys of 'N Sync, shown here with one of their media awards. Hailed as the hottest new group of the year, their U.S. tour was a tremendous success. They were recording songs, winning awards, and television shows clamored for them. The future looked even brighter for the five young men who only want to be one thing: "'N Sync."

climbed to number 34 on the singles chart. (It would later be released as a single.)

Television had not forgotten the group, either. In the month of December alone, the boys were welcome guests on *Live! With Regis & Kathie Lee* and visited with *CBS This Morning*. Specials on which they appeared that month included *Holiday in Concert*, *A Kathie Lee Christmas*, and *Walt Disney World's Very Merry Christmas Parade*.

'N Sync's headlining trek capped the year and would begin the new one of 1999. Following the holiday break, the boys resumed touring in Minnesota before heading west later in January. On another break in February, they worked on their next album. Returning to the road once again in March and April, the group toured with Tatyana Ali.

May 1999 began with new confirmation of the boys' popularity when 'N Sync was honored with the accolade Favorite Group in voting by more than six million kids for Nickelodeon's 12th Annual Kids' Choice Awards. The boys also performed on the show, which was hosted by television personality Rosie O'Donnell.

That same month the group was honored in another, more unusual, way. On May 2, the Caribbean islands of St. Vincent and the Grenadines issued a postage stamp featuring the boys' likenesses. Although most countries do not issue stamps depicting living persons, the island nations are among the few that do.

According to the postmaster of St. Vincent, other entertainers have been depicted in the past. The boys were chosen because they "represented the best of what art and entertainment can present to young people, as they are positive role models with a positive message."

Don't plan on buying the stamps to use on your Christmas cards, however. These special issues, costing one Caribbean dollar each, can only be used on letters or cards mailed from St. Vincent and the Grenadines.

What does the remainder of 1999, and the more distant future, hold for Chris, J.C., Joey, Lance, and Justin? Concert dates were scheduled to fill most of the summer months

In a daring performance at the annual Blockbuster Entertainment Awards in mid-1999, the five thrilled fans when wires lifted them into the air. The ceremony also honored the boys with the Favorite New Group Award.

as the *Boys of Summer* tour made its way across the United States and Canada. Fellow boy band Five and former New Kid on the Block Jordan Knight were slated to tour with 'N Sync. A first-ever trip to Brazil was also on the boys' itinerary.

The group will also continue to be seen on television. Small-screen appearances were scheduled for the *Teen Awards*, *Teenapaloosa*, *Miss Teen USA*, and the *MTV Awards*. In addition, the pay-per-view special *'N Sync 'N Concert* was to air in September.

Obviously, the boys' music is still their foremost concern. They no longer worry about being called a Backstreet Boys clone. They have their own identity, of which they are very proud. As Justin says, "We didn't want to be the next *anybody*. We wanted to be the first 'N Sync."

The group's third album, to which songwriters Diane Warren and David Foster brought their talents, was set for release in October. Both of these artists received 1998 Academy Award nominations, Warren for Aerosmith's "I Don't Want to Miss a Thing" from the film *Armageddon* and Foster for Celine Dion's "The Prayer" from *The Quest for Camelot*. In addition, Justin cowrote one of the tunes for the third album, and J.C. wrote another.

By early summer, the boys' vocal skills were also heard in collaboration with several other artists. In one such partnership, they were to sing backup vocals on the group Alabama's new song—'N Sync's own "God Must Have Spent a Little More Time on You." The track is on Alabama's *20th Century* album.

The boys also recorded a ballad—"Music of My Heart"—together with Gloria Estefan. The

song is featured on the soundtrack of the movie *Music of the Heart*, scheduled for release in the fall of 1999 and starring Meryl Streep, Aidan Quinn, and Estefan. A third project found them teaming up with Phil Collins on the soundtrack of the Disney animated feature *Tarzan*. (They can be heard on the a cappella version of "Trashin' the Camp.")

The silver screen likewise beckons the fabulous quintet. According to one source, the boys will be filming a full-length feature some time in the fall of '99. Reportedly they will be playing roles rather than portraying themselves.

And for 'N Sync fans who can never seem to get enough of the boys, another undertaking is sure to make them sit up and take notice. The group's very own PlayStation video game is on

Although music is their first love, with singles and albums hitting the charts, the boys also have personal plans beyond touring and recording. Television and films beckon, and some business enterprises appear to be in their futures.

the horizon for the near future.

Aside from their work as a group, Chris and Lance have also put in time on their own personal ventures. The boys have talked on occasion about starting their own line of clothes, and Chris has finally done something about it. His Fu-Man Skeeto clothing line, composed of his own creations, was set to debut by 2000.

Lance has gotten into the managing end of the music business, launching Free Lance Entertainment. He oversees the careers of Meredith Edwards and Jack Defeo—two new country singers trying to make their marks. Lance's mother, Diane, and sister, Stacy, head the company, while he pitches in whenever he can. "I do it at night in hotel rooms," he reports. "It's all on the phone."

With a feverish schedule such as theirs, the boys don't have much spare time. When they do, however, each has his own way of spending his downtime. Chris likes most all sports but especially football. He played in high school and says he is pretty good at it now. He also enjoys martial arts and skating. Never tiring of listening to music, Chris has fun attending other groups' concerts.

Unlike Chris, J.C. is not a sports fan. He prefers to spend his spare time with his family, and he would like to have, as he says, "more time to myself." He does enjoy going to the movies, though. It's a way, he explains, to escape from reality for a couple of hours.

In his free time, Joey likes to jet-ski, although he admits he could be better at it. As he says, ". . . I have fun just going fast and turning." He often spends his evenings either going to the movies, sleeping, or enjoying the clubs. Since as a child he was determined to be Superman, it should be no surprise that he is always on the lookout for Superman memorabilia for his large collection.

Like J.C., Lance is not much of a sports fan. He plays basketball once in while with the guys, but says he is "bad" at the game. For Lance, relaxing means enjoying his family and friends or indulging his favorite activity—a day at the beach. "I'm the biggest beach bum," he admits.

For Justin, basketball is his second love, and he plays as often as he can. He is also an avid collector of basketball gear. When not playing, he likes to "just chill" or spend time with his younger brothers.

One thing the boys don't have much time for is dating. It is hard to develop serious relationships when the five are on the road playing nearly 150 concerts a year, making promotional appearances, recording albums, and developing other projects. The boys do, however, have some definite thoughts on what they look for in a girl.

Chris, naturally, looks for a good sense of humor. A young woman who is spontaneous, adventurous, and very outgoing has the best chance of catching his eye. Chris says she should also have "a very beautiful smile. Her eyes and her smile are what say it all for me." Gwen Stefani of No Doubt is his idea of a dream girl. Although he figures he will eventually get married, Chris has no plans to settle down in the immediate future. He is having too much fun living out his dreams and playing the field.

J.C. is serious and hardworking. He never seems to have time to date. When he does

A pleasurable time for the boys of 'N Sync was lending their talents to the Miss Teen USA pageant. The guys obviously enjoy being surrounded by young women, but their hectic schedule leaves them little time for long-term relationships.

get the chance, he looks for someone who can help him relax and make him laugh. She must also be patient, however, since J.C. is extremely serious about succeeding in the music business that makes up such a large part of his life. Rather than being a party animal, like Chris, Joey, or Justin, J.C.'s idea of an enjoyable evening is a quiet, romantic dinner, possibly followed by an entertaining show. Although looks are not the most important thing to him, he does admit that the first thing he notices about a girl are her eyes and her lips.

As the most talkative and flirtatious member of the group, Joey is nicknamed "Chick Magnet" by Chris. He is attracted to young women who are friendly and confident and who can match his action on the dance floor. It also helps if a chosen one can cook; Joey has been spoiled by his mom's Italian cuisine.

One of the girls Joey has paired off with recently is Lene Crawford Nystrom, a singer in the Swedish band Aqua. "Lene is very attractive and sexy," says Joey, "and I love her sense of humor." Unfortunately, with both of them so committed to, and involved with, their respective groups, there has not yet been time for the relationship to reach the serious stage.

Always the gentleman, Lance has been nicknamed "Stealth" by the others because of the way he can quietly and quickly sweep a girl right off her feet. The sweet, innocent, wholesome, all-American girl is his ideal. She should also be the outdoors type, able to enjoy horseback riding, hiking, and the beach. If the girl is daring enough to go for something more adventurous, like parasailing, so much the better. One of the girls who has spent a good deal of time with Lance recently is Danielle Fishel, who plays the part of Topanga on *Boy Meets World.*

Like all of the others, Justin thinks personality in a girl is much more important than looks. "I like a girl with a good sense of humor, who's humble, and sensitive," says the youngest member of 'N Sync. The group's "Mr. Smooth" looks for self-confidence in his dates but not cockiness. He hopes some day to find a girl who will simply like him for *who* he is rather than *what* he is. Singer Britney Spears, a fellow *Mickey Mouse Club* alumna, is a young lady rumored to be the current love interest of the blond, curly-haired heartthrob.

What the more distant future holds for the ambitious boys still remains to be seen. All of them fully realize that fame can be a fleeting thing. "We could be gone next year," says Chris, "and people won't have a clue who we were." Having been involved in show business for several years now, there is a good possibility they may spend more time in the writing or production part of the industry. J.C. in particular often pictures himself in some behind-the-scenes capacity, such as being an engineer or producer.

Whatever the future may bring, there is one thing of which admirers can be sure: 'N Sync plans on bringing pleasure to its millions of fans for years to come, and the five will do it their way. "We want to be pioneers in the music industry," says Justin. "We want to make our own name. We have inspiration individually and as a group . . . but we just want to be 'N Sync." Millions of fans around the world could ask for nothing more.

CHRONOLOGY

1971   Christopher Alan Kirkpatrick born on October 17 in Clarion, Pennsylvania.

1976   Joshua Scott Chasez born on August 8 in Washington, D.C.

1977   Joseph Anthony Fatone Jr. born on January 28 in Brooklyn, New York.

1979   James Lance Bass born on May 4 in Clinton, Mississippi.

1981   Justin Randall Timberlake born on January 31 in Memphis, Tennessee.

1995   'N Sync formed by Chris Kirkpatrick.

1996   Johnny Wright becomes 'N Sync's manager; sign recording contract with BMG Ariola Munich, Germany; release "I Want You Back" and "Tearin' Up My Heart" in Germany; tour Germany.

1997   Release album *'N Sync* in Germany; tour Europe, Asia, and Australia.

1998   Release "I Want You Back" and "Tearin' Up My Heart" in U.S.; release *'N Sync* in U.S.; film *In Concert* Special for Disney Channel at Walt Disney World; tour U.S.; release *Home for Christmas* in U.S.

1999   Win two *Billboard* Music Video Awards, Best Clip of the Year and Best New Artist Clip of the Year; 'N Sync stamp issued by islands of St. Vincent and the Grenadines; voted Favorite Group at 12th Annual Nickelodeon's Kids' Choice Awards; tour U.S. and Canada; record third album.

ACCOMPLISHMENTS

Singles (U.S.)

1998   "I Want You Back"

"Tearin' Up My Heart"

"Merry Christmas, Happy Holidays"

1999   "God Must Have Spent a Little More Time on You"

Albums (U.S.)

1998   *'N Sync*

Home for Christmas

Major television appearances (U.S.)

1998   *'N Sync in Concert*

The Late Show with David Letterman

The Tonight Show with Jay Leno

Live! With Regis & Kathie Lee

CBS This Morning

Ricki Lake

Holiday in Concert

Walt Disney World's Very Merry Christmas Parade

A Kathie Lee Christmas

1999   *Nickelodeon's 12th Annual Kids' Choice Awards*

FURTHER READING

Golden, Anna Louise. *'N Sync: An Unauthorized Biography.* New York: St. Martin's, 1999.

Johns, Michael-Anne. *'N Sync—Backstage Pass: Your Kickin' Keepsake Scrapbook!* New York: Scholastic, 1999.

Kelman, Chris. *'N Sync.* New York: Andrews McMeel Publishing, 1999.

Krulik, Nancy E. *'N Sync with J.C.* New York: Pocket Books, 1999.

Netter, Matt. *'N Sync: Tearin' Up the Charts.* New York: Pocket Books, 1998.

Netter, Matt. *'N Sync with Justin.* New York: Pocket Books, 1999.

Nichols, Angie. *'N Sync.* London: Virgin Books, 1998.

'N Sync with K.M. Squires. *'N Sync: The Official Book.* New York: Bantam Doubleday Dell, 1998.

INDEX